# DEMI'S
# FIND THE ANIMAL
# A·B·C

*For Eliza Hitz*
*who drew this horse*

## How to Play

Look closely at the drawing of the small unicorn in the box
on the facing page. Then find that little unicorn somewhere in
the drawing of the big unicorn. Play this Find-the-Animal game
on every page. Answers to the picture puzzles are given at the
end of the book.

# DEMI'S
# FIND THE ANIMAL
# A·B·C

## an alphabet-game book

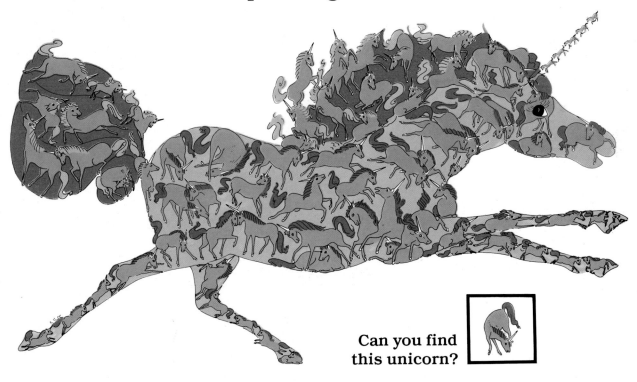

**Can you find this unicorn?**

## GROSSET & DUNLAP

Copyright © 1985 by Demi. All rights reserved. Published by
Grosset & Dunlap, Inc., a member of The Putnam Publishing Group,
New York. Published simultaneously in Canada. Printed in Hong Kong.
Library of Congress Catalog Card Number: 85-70285
ISBN 0-448-18970-4     D E F G H I J

1990 Paperback Edition    ISBN 0-448-19165-2

# Aa

Can you find
this alligator?

# Bb

Can you find
this bird?

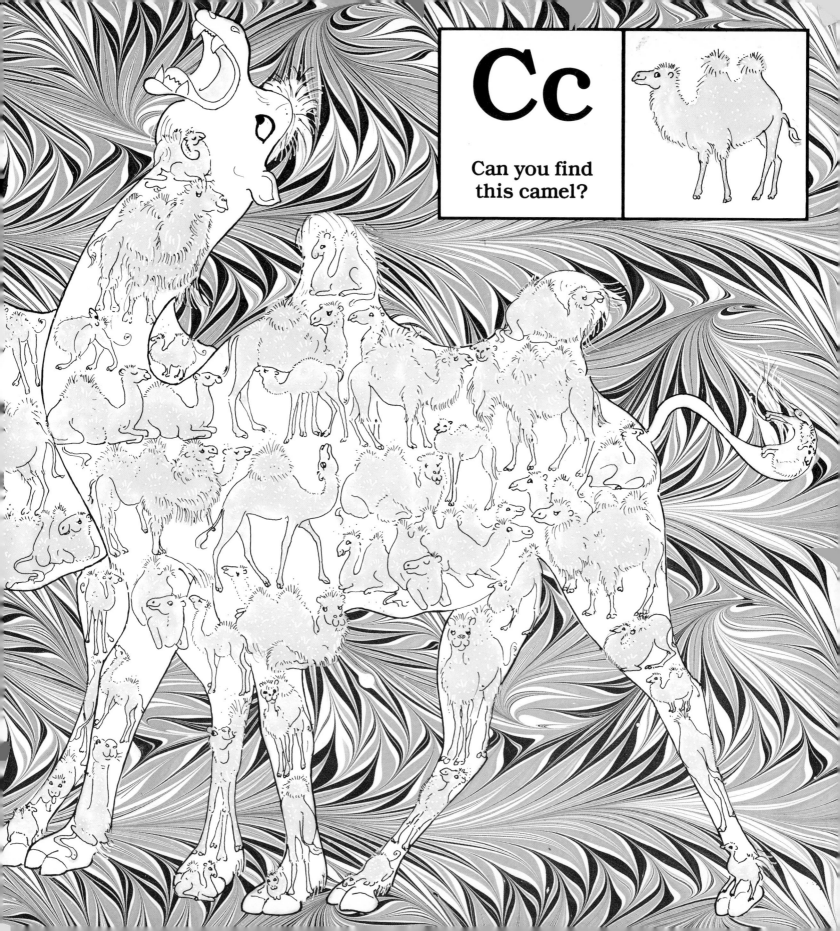

# Cc

Can you find
this camel?

# Dd

**Can you find this dog?**

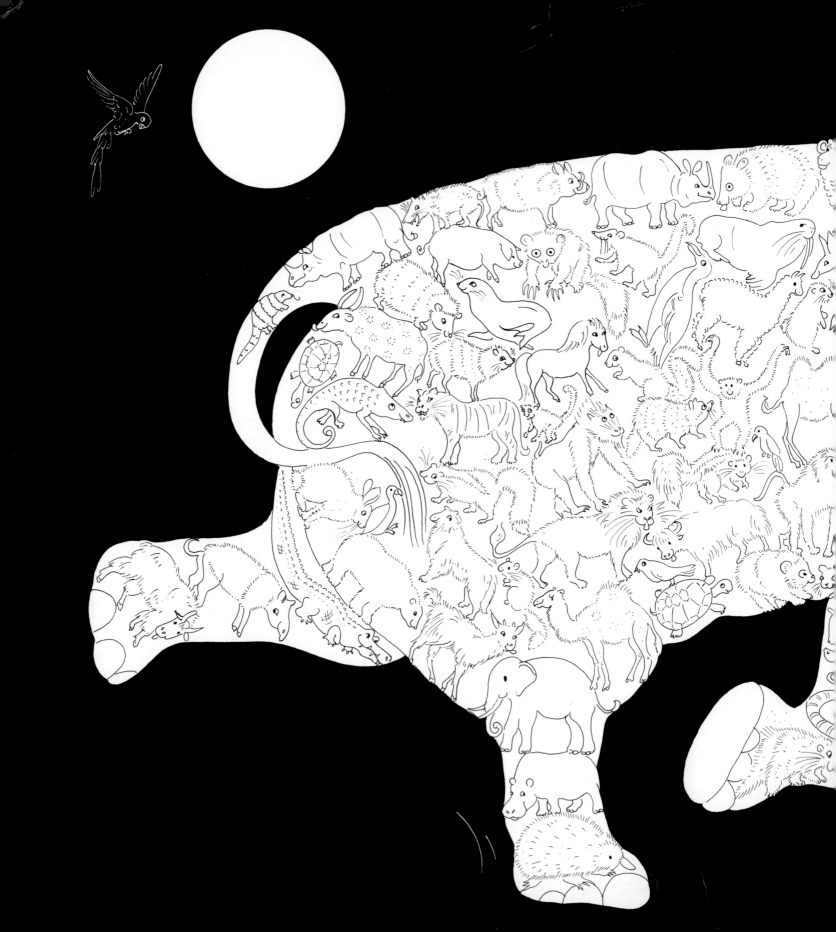

**Ee**

Can you find
this elephant?

# Ff

Can you find
this fox?

**Gg**

Can you find
this giraffe?

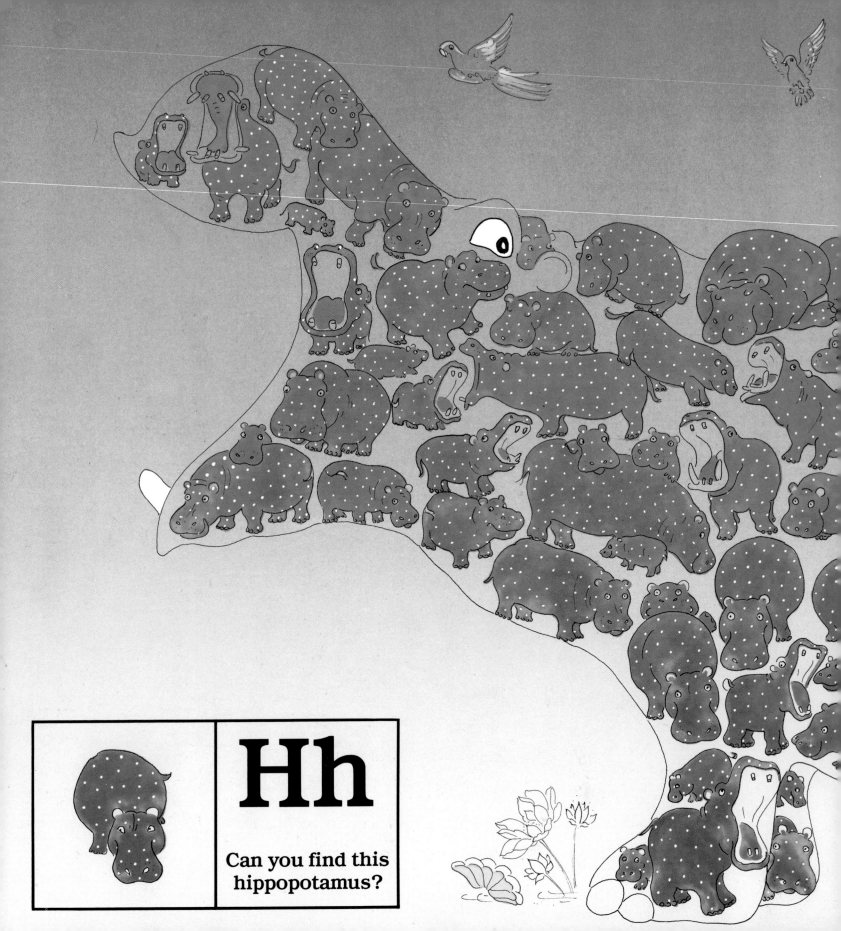

# Hh

Can you find this hippopotamus?

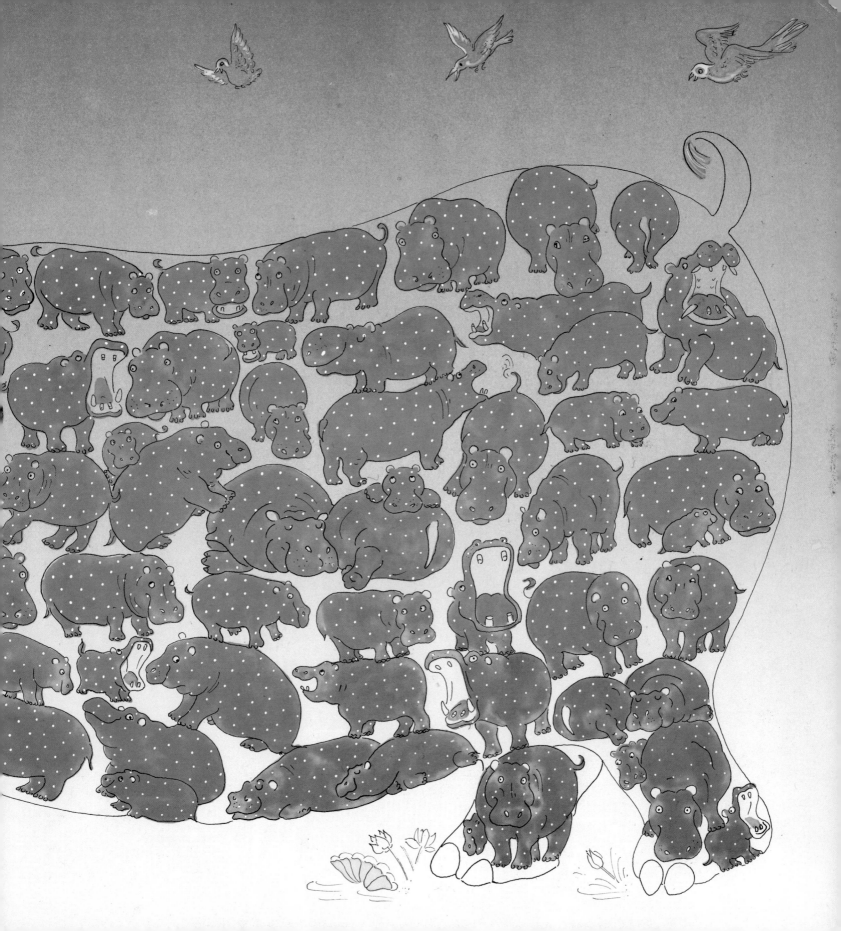

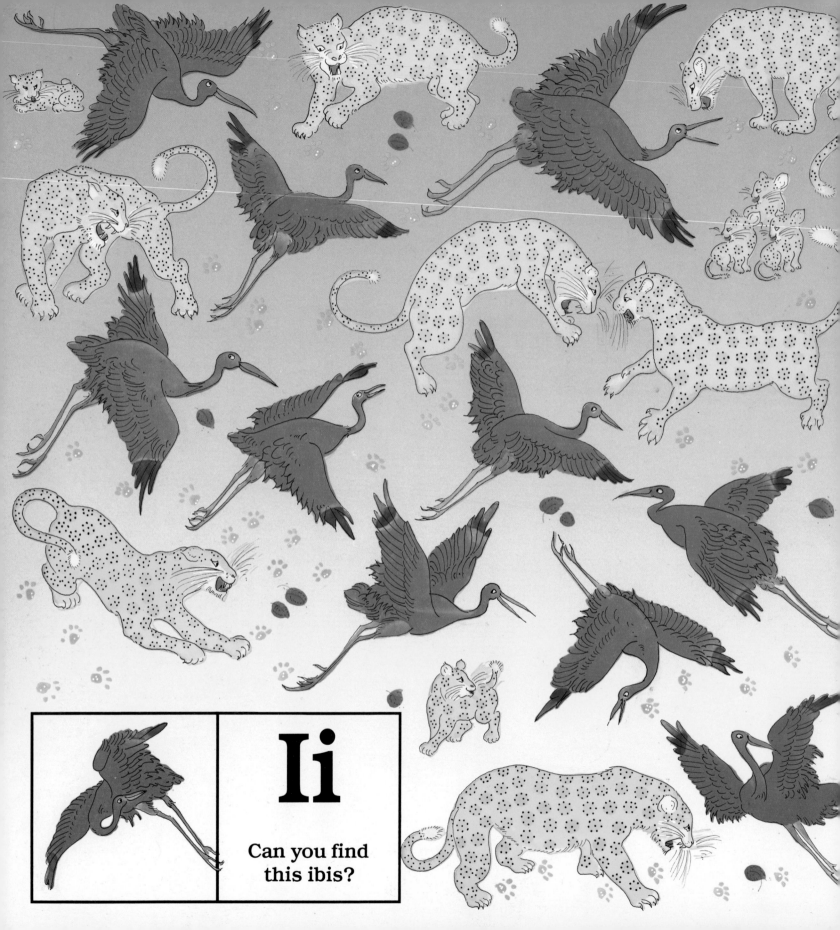

# Ii

Can you find
this ibis?

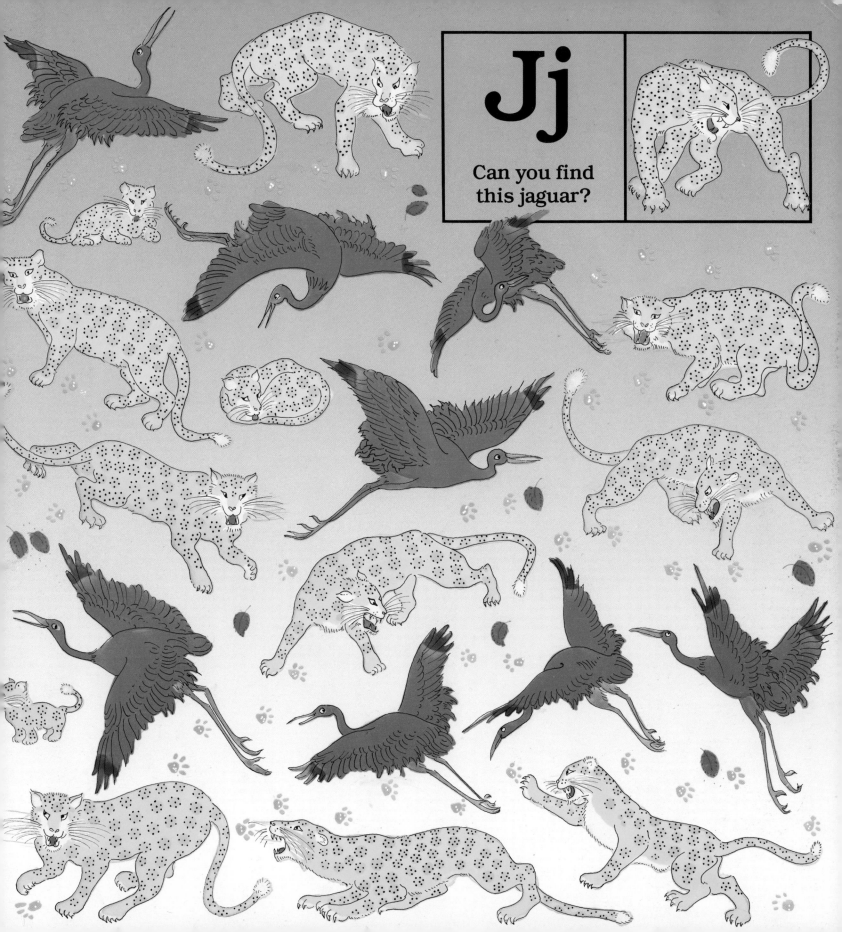

# Jj

**Can you find this jaguar?**

# Kk

Can you find
this kangaroo?

# L l

Can you find
this lion?

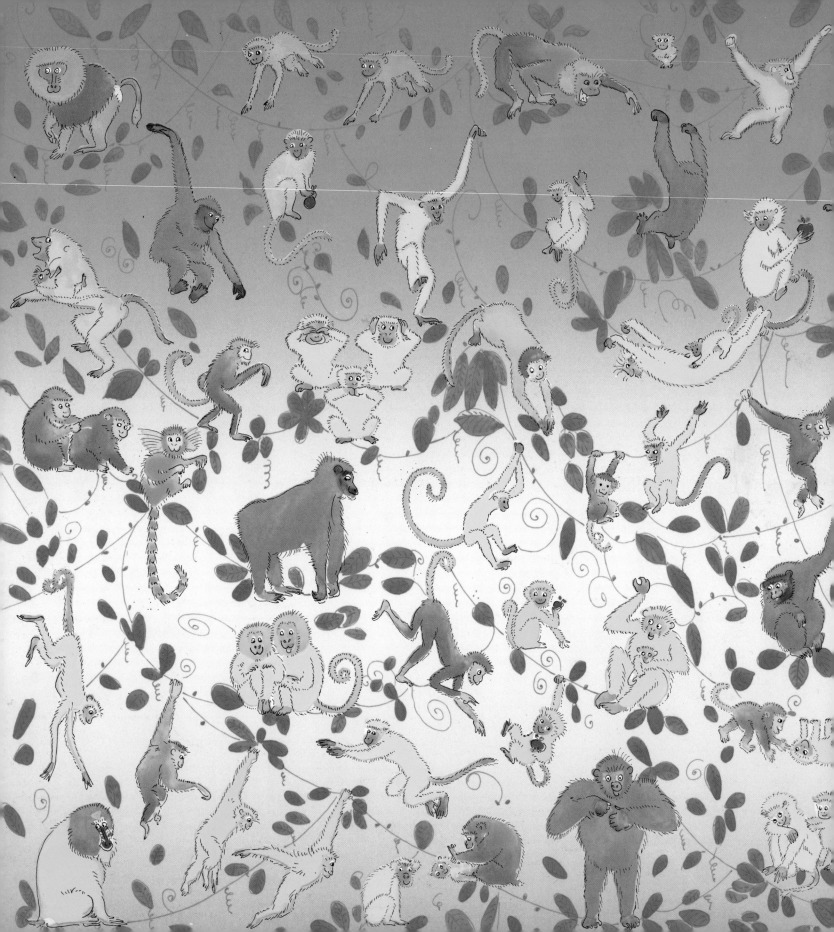

# Mm

Can you find
this monkey?

# Nn

Can you find
this nine-banded
armadillo?

**Oo**

Can you find this ostrich?

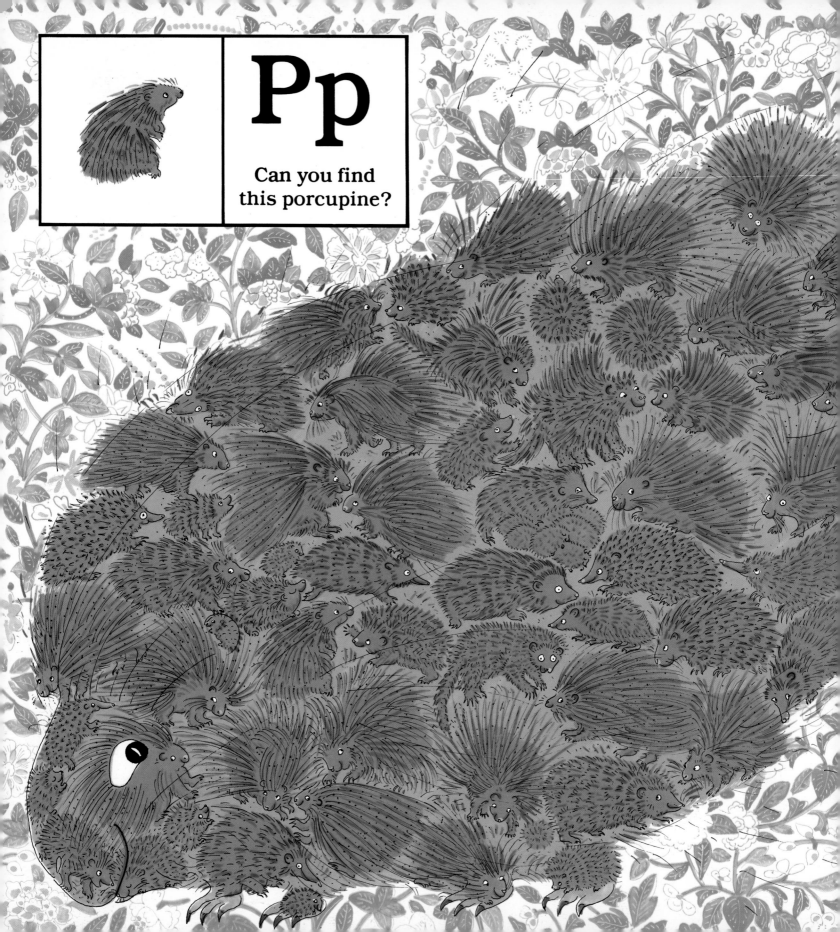

# Pp

Can you find
this porcupine?

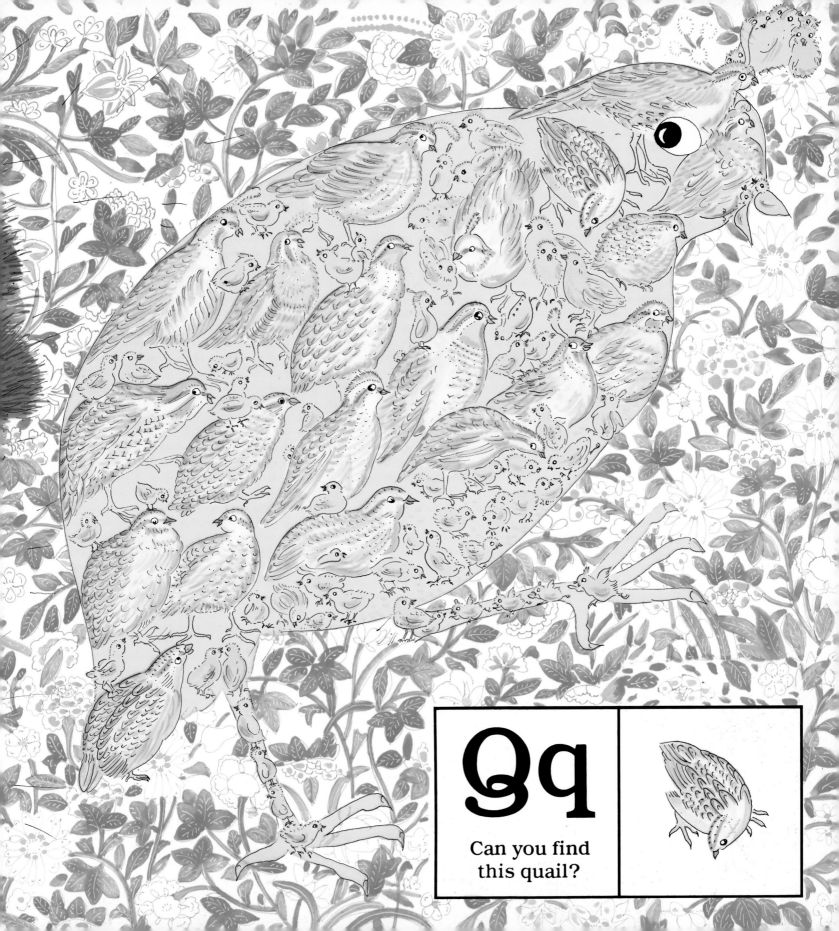

**Qq**

Can you find
this quail?

# Rr

**Can you find
this rabbit?**

RABBIT.

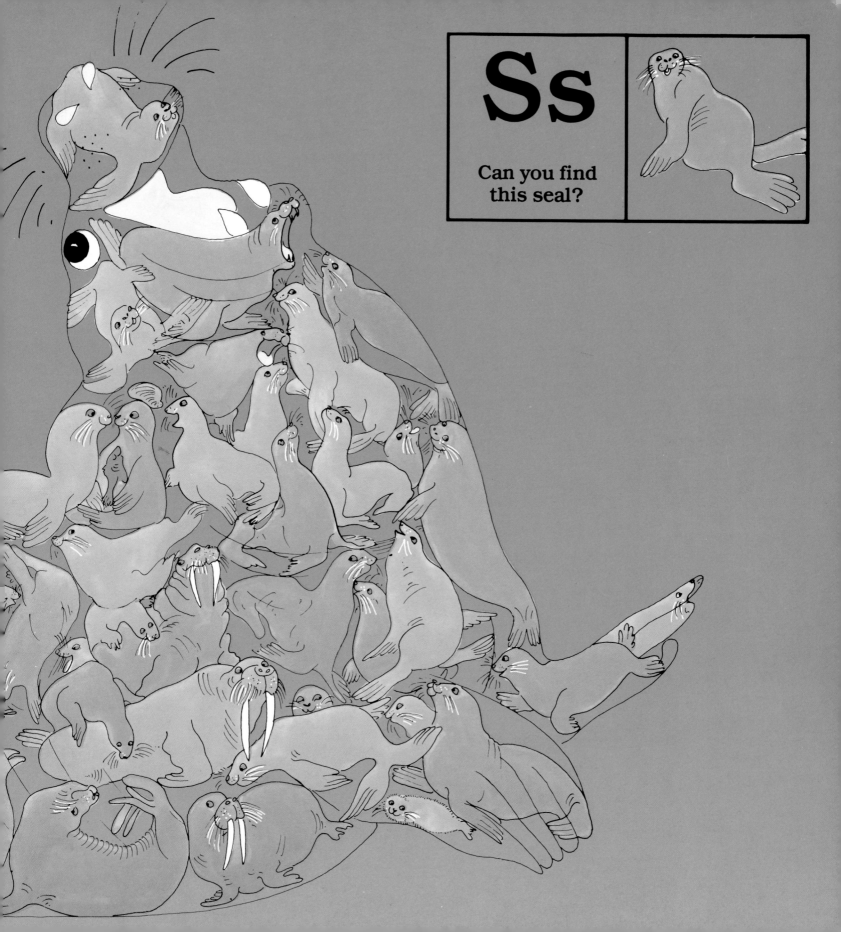

**Ss**

Can you find
this seal?

TURTLE
RACE

# Tt

**Can you find this turtle?**

FINISH

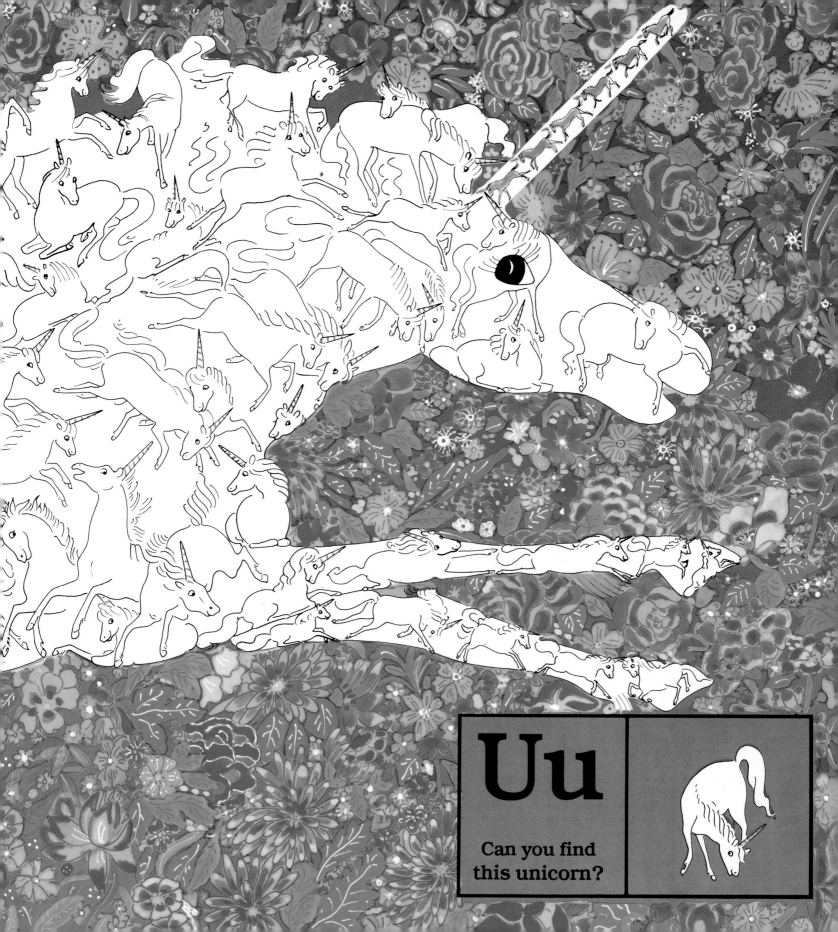

**Uu**

Can you find
this unicorn?

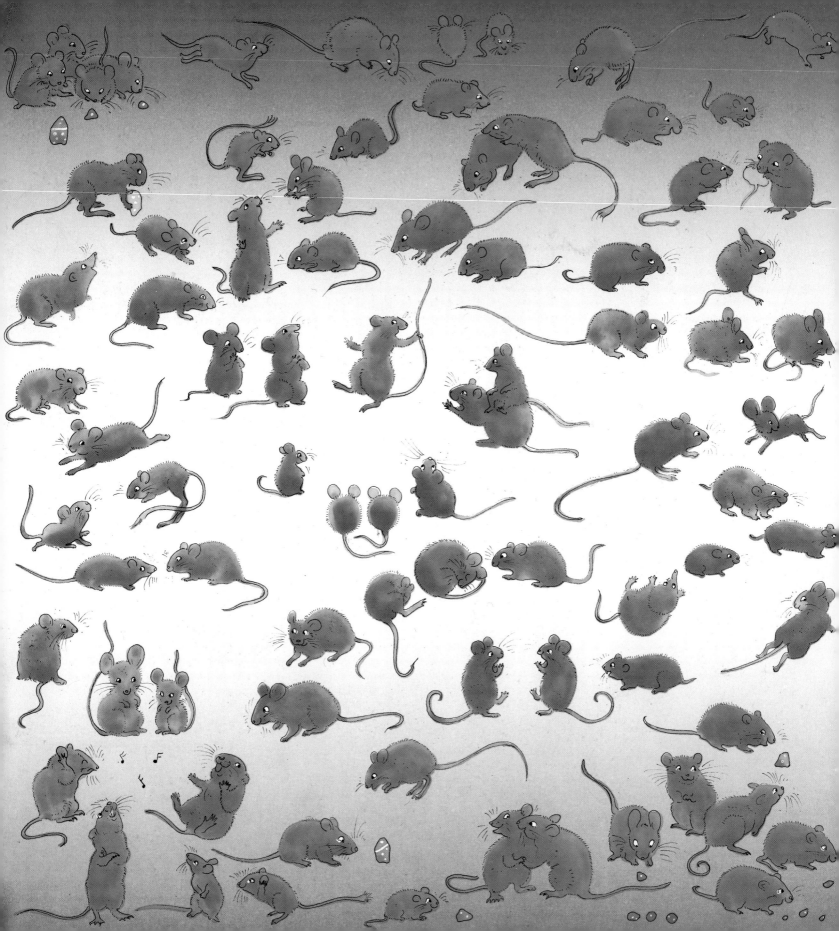

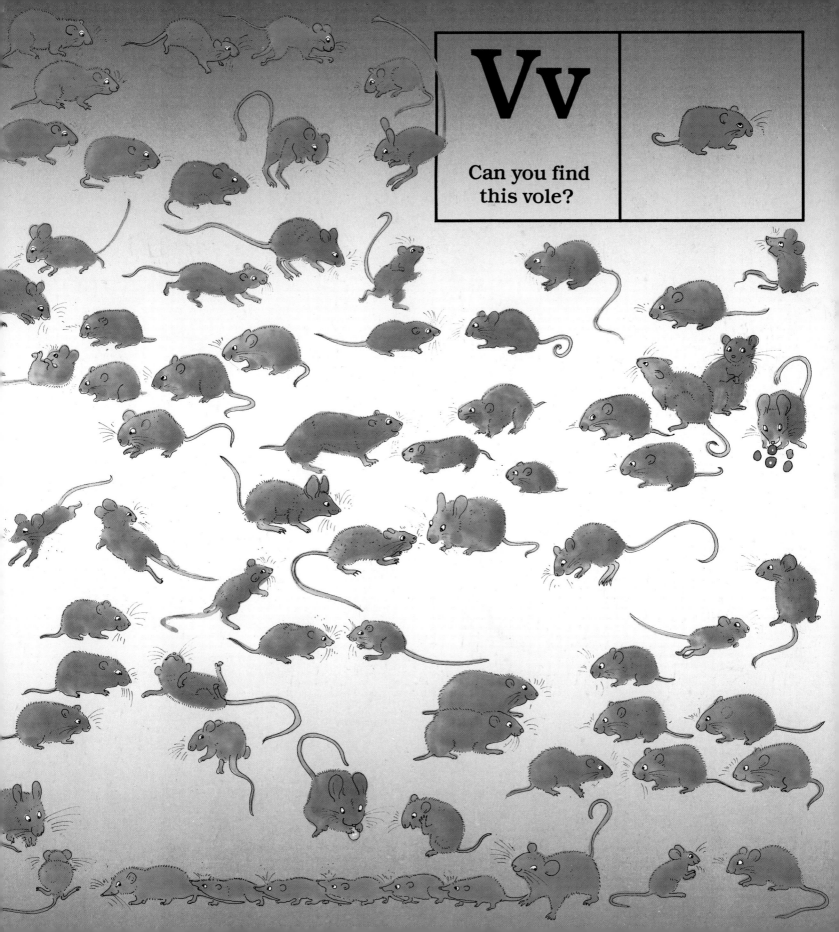

# Vv

Can you find
this vole?

# Ww

**Can you find this whale?**

# Xx

Can you find
the X-ray fish?

# Yy

Can you find
this yak?

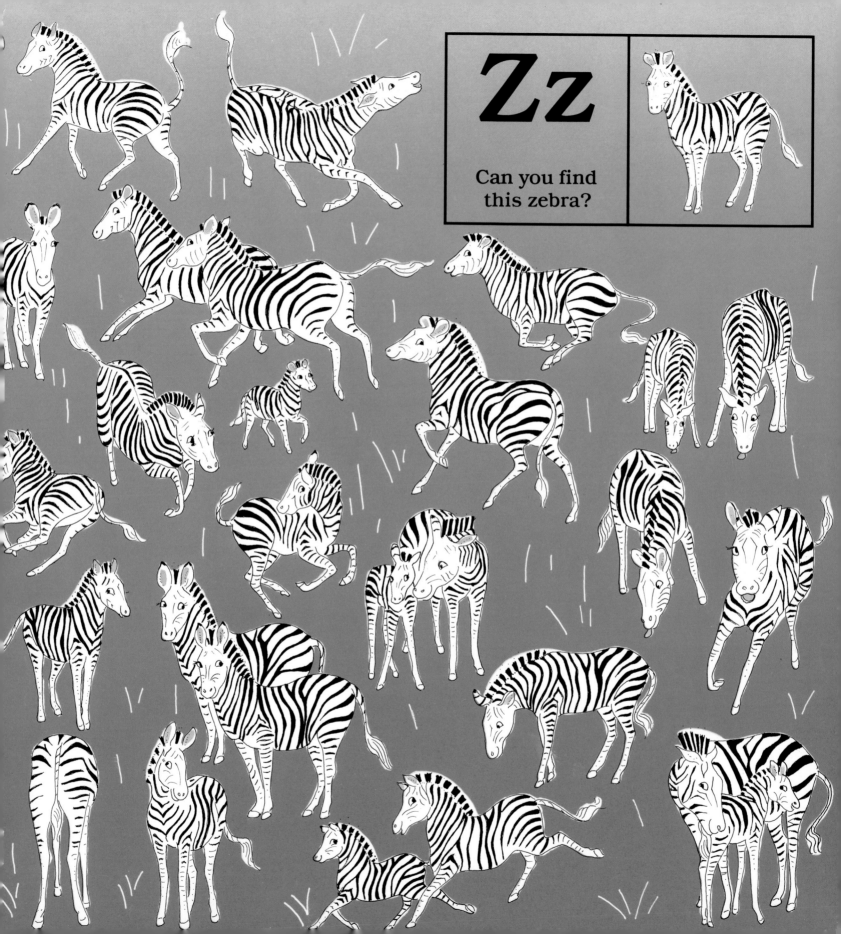

# Zz

**Can you find this zebra?**

# ANSWERS

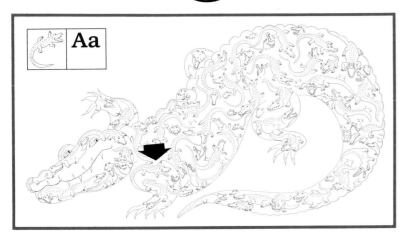

Alligator

Bird

Camel

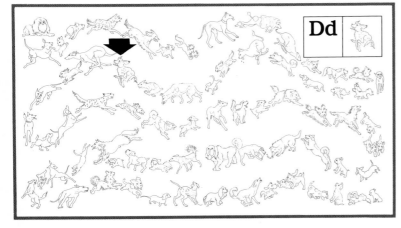

Dog

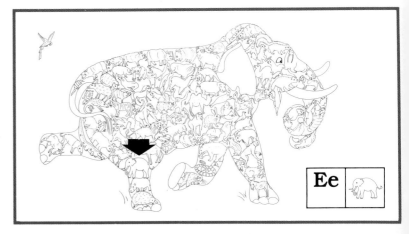

Elephant

Fox and Giraffe

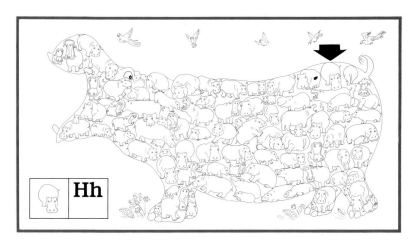

Hippopotamus

Ibis and Jaguar

Kangaroo and Lion

Monkey

**Nine-banded Armadillo and Ostrich**

**Porcupine and Quail**

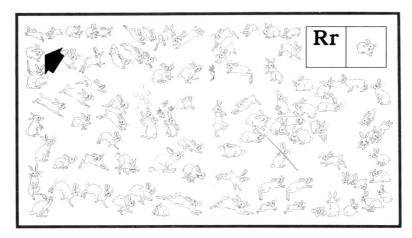

**Rabbit**

**Seal**

**Turtle**

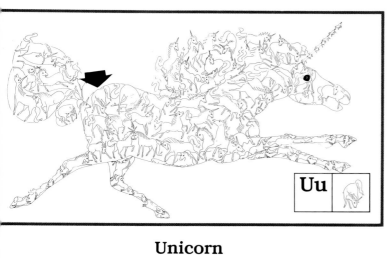

Unicorn

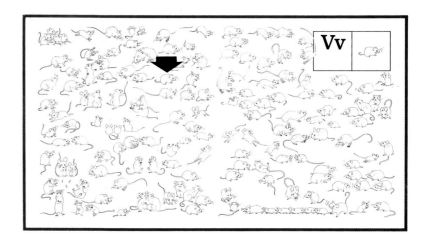

Vole

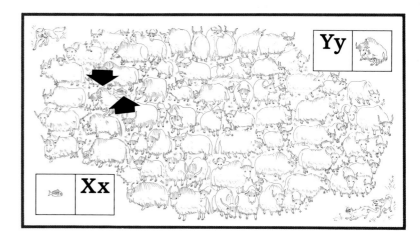

Whale

X-ray Fish and Yak

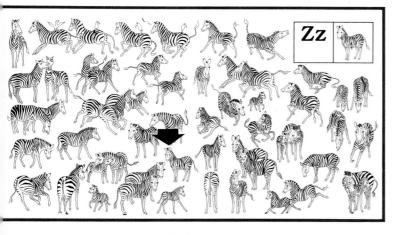

Zebra

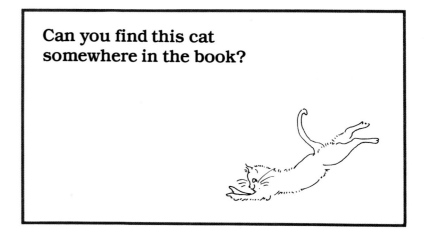

Can you find this cat
somewhere in the book?